Copyright 2014, Gooseberry Patch
First Printing, February, 2014

Juicy burgers start with ground beef chuck. A little fat in the beef adds flavor...there's no need to pay more for extra-lean ground sirloin!

Bestest Burger Ever

Makes 6 sandwiches

2 lbs. ground beef
1 onion, chopped
1 t. salt
1 t. pepper
1 t. dried basil
1/3 c. teriyaki sauce

1/4 c. Italian seasoned bread
  crumbs
1 T. grated Parmesan cheese
6 slices American cheese
6 onion rolls, split

Mix together beef, onion, salt, pepper and basil. Add teriyaki sauce, bread crumbs and Parmesan cheese; mix well. Divide into 6 patties. Grill to desired doneness; top with American cheese. Serve on onion rolls.

Tuck burgers into the pockets of halved pita rounds...
easy for small hands to hold and a tasty change
from the same old hamburger buns.

4

Italian Hamburgers

Makes 12 to 14 servings

2 to 3 slices bacon, crisply cooked
    and crumbled
3 lbs. ground beef
0.7-oz. pkg. Italian salad dressing
    mix

2 eggs, beaten
1 c. Italian-flavored dry bread
    crumbs
1 c. shredded mozzarella cheese
12 to 14 hamburger buns, split

In a large bowl, combine all ingredients except buns. Mix well and form into 12 to 14 patties. Grill to preferred doneness. Serve on buns.

Savor sweet onions when they're in season from April to August!
Often named for the region where they're grown, like Vidalia,
Walla Walla, Maui Sweets and Bermuda, sweet onions are mild,
crisp and especially delicious eaten uncooked on grilled
burgers, sandwiches and tossed salads.

Mini Onion Burgers

1 red onion, sliced
1 lb. lean ground beef
1/4 t. salt
1/8 t. pepper
12 to 15 small potato rolls, split

6 T. mayonnaise
2 T. Dijon mustard
1/2 to 1 t. cayenne pepper
Optional: mustard, catsup or
    mayonnaise

Preheat a flat-top grill pan over high heat. Add onion and cook until tender, about 10 minutes; remove to a bowl. In a separate bowl, mix beef, salt and pepper. Form into small patties, about 2 inches across. Add patties to grill pan; cook 3 to 4 minutes per side. For Special Sauce, mix mayonnaise, mustard and cayenne pepper in a small bowl. Serve patties on buns with grilled onion, Special Sauce and other toppings, if desired.

Slip your hands inside 2 plastic bags when shaping
ground beef into burgers...no more messy hands!

8

Best-Ever Cheddar Burgers

Serves 4

1 to 1-1/2 lbs. ground turkey
4 green onions, finely chopped
1/3 c. fresh parsley, chopped
1 T. grill seasoning
1 t. poultry seasoning
2 T. oil
1 Granny Smith apple, cored and
thinly sliced

8 slices Cheddar cheese
1/4 c. whole-berry cranberry
sauce
2 T. spicy brown mustard
4 buns, split and toasted
8 leaves green leaf lettuce

Combine turkey, onions, parsley and seasonings; form into 4 patties.
Heat oil in a skillet over medium-high heat. Add patties and cook
5 minutes per side, or until no longer pink in the center. Arrange 2 to
3 apple slices and 2 cheese slices over each patty. Remove skillet from
heat; cover to let cheese melt. Blend cranberry sauce and mustard
together; spread on cut sides of buns. Add lettuce and burgers;
close sandwiches.

Store unwashed, dry mushrooms in the refrigerator.
The mushrooms will stay fresher longer if they're placed
in a paper bag rather than a plastic bag.

Irene's Portabella Burgers

4 portabella mushroom caps
1 c. Italian salad dressing
4 sourdough buns, split

4 slices Muenster or Gruyère
  cheese
Garnish: romaine lettuce

Combine mushrooms and salad dressing in a plastic zipping bag, turning to coat. Chill 30 minutes, turning occasionally. Remove mushrooms, discarding dressing. Grill mushrooms, covered with grill lid, over medium heat for 2 to 3 minutes on each side. Grill buns, cut-side down, one minute, or until toasted. Top buns with mushroom, cheese and lettuce; serve immediately.

Make a quick condiment kit for your next backyard barbecue.
Just place salt, pepper, mustard, catsup, flatware and napkins
in an empty cardboard pop carrier...so easy!

Deviled Hamburgers

1 lb. ground beef
2 T. catsup
1 T. onion, chopped
2 t. mustard

1 t. red steak sauce
1 t. seasoned salt
1/2 t. pepper
4 hamburger buns, split

In the morning, mix together all ingredients except buns; form into
4 patties. Cover and refrigerate until evening. Cook to desired doneness
as you prefer by frying in a skillet, or grilling on a countertop grill or an
outdoor grill. Serve burgers on buns.

Traveling a distance to your cookout site? Wrap and freeze burgers or marinated meat before packing in an ice chest. The frozen meat will help keep other items cold and will thaw in time for grilling.

Bacon-Stuffed Burgers

4 slices bacon, crisply cooked,
    crumbled and drippings
    reserved
1/4 c. onion, chopped
4-oz. can mushroom pieces,
    drained and diced
1 lb. ground beef

1 lb. ground pork sausage
1/4 c. grated Parmesan cheese
1/2 t. pepper
1/2 t. garlic powder
2 T. steak sauce
8 sandwich buns, split
Optional: lettuce

Heat 2 tablespoons reserved drippings in a skillet over medium heat.
Add onion and sauté until tender. Add cooked bacon and mushrooms;
heat through and set aside. Combine beef, sausage, cheese, pepper, garlic
powder and steak sauce in a large bowl. Shape into 16 thin patties.
Spoon bacon mixture over 8 patties. Place remaining patties on top and
press edges tightly to seal. Grill over medium coals to desired doneness.
Serve on buns with lettuce, if desired.

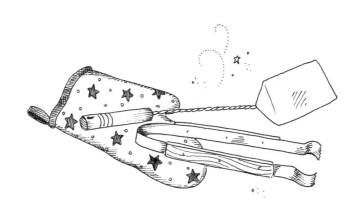

For the juiciest foods, flip grilled burgers with a spatula and turn steaks or chicken with tongs, not a fork. The holes a fork makes will let the juices escape.

Gobblin' Good Turkey Burgers *Makes 4 to 6 sandwiches*

1 lb. ground turkey
1 onion, minced
1 c. shredded Cheddar cheese
1/4 c. Worcestershire sauce

1/2 t. dry mustard
salt and pepper to taste
4 to 6 hamburger buns, split

Combine all ingredients except buns; form into 4 to 6 patties. Grill to desired doneness; serve on hamburger buns.

Hollowed-out peppers make garden-fresh servers for catsup, relish and mustard! Just cut a slice off the bottom so they'll sit flat.

Prosciutto Burgers

Makes 6 burgers

1 to 1-1/2 lbs. ground beef
1/2 c. dry bread crumbs
1 to 2 t. dried parsley
1 egg, beaten
2 T. milk
1/2 c. grated Parmesan cheese
1/4 c. sun-dried tomatoes,
    chopped

3/4 t. salt
3/4 t. pepper
6 slices prosciutto ham
1/4 c. olive oil
6 hamburger buns, split
6 slices tomato
Garnish: grated Parmesan cheese

In a large bowl, mix together beef, bread crumbs, parsley, egg, milk, cheese, sun-dried tomatoes, salt and pepper. Form mixture into 6 patties. Wrap each patty with a slice of prosciutto. Heat oil in a large skillet over medium heat. Fry patties in oil for 3 to 4 minutes per side, until prosciutto is crisp and burgers reach desired doneness. Serve each burger on a bun, topped with a slice of tomato and sprinkled with Parmesan cheese.

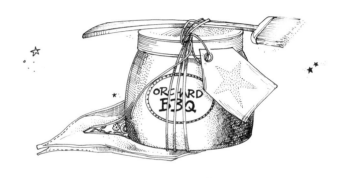

Use a length of jute to tie a basting brush to the top of
a jar of Norma's BBQ Sauce, then slip the jar into
an oven mitt or apron pocket...so clever!

Norma's BBQ Sauce

Makes 13 one-quart bottles

6 c. onions, chopped
3 c. margarine
12-oz. pkg. all-purpose flour
6 c. vinegar
1/4 c. hot pepper sauce
4 qts. water
1-1/4 c. Worcestershire sauce

2-1/2 t. pepper
8 qts. catsup
1 c. chili powder
1-1/2 lbs. brown sugar
1 c. mustard
13 1-quart catsup bottles and
    lids, sterilized

In a large skillet over medium heat, cook together onions and margarine until warmed through; whisk in flour. Cook until onions are tender; place in a very large stockpot. Add remaining ingredients; increase heat to medium-high and bring to a boil. Pour into sterilized catsup bottles, leaving 1/4-inch headspace; wipe rims. Secure with sterilized lids; set aside to cool to room temperature. May keep in the freezer up to one year; thaw to use.

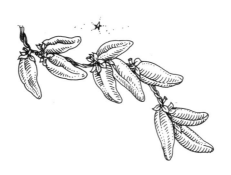

When making any dish with hot jalapeño peppers, it's always a good idea to wear plastic gloves to avoid irritation while cutting, slicing and chopping. Don't touch your face, lips or eyes while you're working! Just toss away the gloves when you're done.

Spicy Butter Bean Burgers

Serves 4

15-oz. can butter beans or
    lima beans, drained
1/2 c. onion, chopped
1 T. jalapeño pepper, finely
    chopped and seeds removed
6 to 8 saltine crackers, crushed
1 egg, beaten

1/2 c. shredded Cheddar cheese
1/4 t. garlic powder
salt and pepper to taste
olive oil for frying
4 whole-wheat sandwich
    buns, split

Mash beans in a bowl; mix in remaining ingredients except oil and buns.
Form into 4 patties. Add 1/4 inch oil to a skillet over medium-high heat.
Fry patties until golden, about 5 minutes per side, turning carefully.
If baking is preferred, place patties on a greased baking sheet; bake at
400 degrees for 7 to 10 minutes per side. Serve on buns.

Charcoal or gas? Every cookout chef has
her own definite opinion. A good rule of thumb:
charcoal is for taste and gas is for haste.

All-In-One Bacon Cheeseburgers   *Makes 6 servings*

1-1/2 lbs. lean ground beef
1-oz. pkg. ranch salad
    dressing mix
3-oz. jar bacon bits

8-oz. pkg. finely shredded
    Italian-blend cheese
6 hamburger buns, split

Place beef in a large bowl. Mix in remaining ingredients, one at a time, except buns. Form into 6 patties. Grill burgers for 3 to 4 minutes per side, or to desired doneness. Serve on buns.

A big shaker of seasoning salt is a must-have for tasty grilling.
Mix up your very own blend! A good basic mixture is a teaspoon
each of salt, pepper, garlic powder and oregano or rosemary.
Like it spicy? Add some cayenne pepper or dry mustard.

26

Crunchy Chicken Burgers

Serves 4 to 6

1 lb. ground chicken
1/4 c. honey barbecue sauce
3/4 c. mini shredded wheat
   cereal, crushed

1 egg, beaten
1/8 t. salt
1/8 t. pepper
4 to 6 hamburger buns, split

Mix all ingredients together except buns; form into 4 to 6 patties.
Grill for 5 to 6 minutes per side, until no longer pink in the center. Serve
on buns.

Light and fizzy...the perfect drink for a cookout! Combine one cup sugar, 6 cups chilled pineapple juice and one cup lime juice. Stir in 2 liters sparkling water and serve over crushed ice.

Aloha Burgers

8-oz. can pineapple slices,
  drained and juice reserved
3/4 c. teriyaki sauce
1 lb. ground beef
1 T. butter, softened

4 hamburger buns, split
4 slices Swiss cheese
4 slices bacon, crisply cooked
4 leaves lettuce
1 red onion, sliced

Stir together reserved pineapple juice and teriyaki sauce in a small bowl. Place pineapple slices and 3 tablespoons juice mixture into a plastic zipping bag. Turn to coat; set aside. Shape ground beef into 4 patties and spoon remaining juice mixture over top; set aside. Spread butter on buns; set aside. Grill patties over medium-high heat to desired doneness, turning to cook on both sides. Place buns on grill, cut-side down, to toast lightly. Remove pineapple slices from plastic bag; place on grill and heat through until lightly golden, about one minute per side. Serve burgers on buns topped with pineapple, cheese, bacon, lettuce and onion.

Don't toss that almost-empty Dijon mustard jar! Use it to
mix up a zesty salad dressing. Pour 3 tablespoons olive oil,
2 tablespoons cider vinegar and a clove of minced garlic into
the jar, replace the lid and shake well. Add salt and pepper
to taste. Drizzle over mixed greens...so refreshing.

Garlic & Mustard Burgers

Serves 4

1 lb. ground beef
3 T. country-style Dijon mustard
5 garlic cloves, chopped
4 hamburger buns, split

4 Monterey Jack cheese slices
7-oz. jar roasted red peppers,
   drained

Mix together beef, mustard and garlic. Shape into 4 patties about
3/4-inch thick. Cover and grill patties for 12 to 15 minutes total, to
desired doneness. Top burgers with cheese and peppers.

Mini burgers are fun for parties...thriftier than
full-size sandwiches too, since everyone can take just what
they want! Use mini brown & serve rolls for buns.

Incredible Mini Burger Bites *Makes 24 mini sandwiches*

2 lbs. lean ground beef
1-1/2 oz. pkg. onion soup mix
2 eggs, beaten
1/2 c. dry bread crumbs
3 T. water
1/2 t. garlic salt
1 t. pepper

24 dinner rolls, split
6 slices American cheese,
    quartered
Garnish: catsup, mustard,
    shredded lettuce, thinly sliced
    onion, dill pickles

In a bowl, mix beef, soup mix, eggs, bread crumbs, water and spices; refrigerate for one hour. Spread beef mixture on a greased 15"x10" jelly-roll pan. Cover with plastic wrap and roll out evenly with a rolling pin. Discard plastic wrap; bake at 400 degrees for 12 minutes. Slice into 24 squares with a pizza cutter. Top each roll with a burger square, a cheese slice and desired garnishes.

No more flimsy paper plates at the next potluck...they'll fit
nice and snug inside a plastic flying disc. After lunch,
it makes a terrific gift for everyone to take home!

Bean & Chile Burgers

Makes 4 servings

16-oz. can black beans, drained
    and rinsed
11-oz. can corn, drained
4-oz. can green chiles
1 c. cooked rice
1/2 c. cornmeal
1 t. onion powder
1/4 t. garlic powder
salt to taste
2 T. oil
4 sandwich buns, split
Optional: salsa

Mash beans in a large bowl; add corn, chiles, rice, cornmeal, onion powder and garlic powder. Form mixture into 4 large patties; sprinkle with salt. Heat oil in a skillet over medium heat; add patties and cook until golden on both sides. Serve on buns, topped with salsa, if desired.

Help the kids set up a summertime lemonade stand!
Make a booth from old appliance boxes or push two card
tables together...neighbors will line up to enjoy
icy glasses of freshly-squeezed lemonade!

Beverly's Bacon Burgers

3 lbs. ground beef
2 potatoes, peeled and chopped
4 carrots, peeled and grated
1 onion, grated
2 eggs, beaten
1-1/2 t. garlic, minced

1 to 2 t. dried parsley
1 t. salt
pepper to taste
14 slices bacon
14 sandwich buns, split

Mix together all ingredients except bacon and buns; form into 14 patties.
Wrap a bacon slice around each patty and secure with a wooden
toothpick. Grill or broil to desired doneness. Serve on buns.

Pick up a stack of diner-style plastic burger baskets. Lined with
checked paper napkins, they're lots of fun for serving burgers,
hot dogs and fries. Don't forget to add a pickle spear!

Diner-Style Burgers

Makes 8 servings

2 lbs. ground beef
1 egg, beaten
1 c. onion, finely chopped
1/2 c. shredded Cheddar cheese
2 T. catsup
2 T. evaporated milk

1/2 c. cracker crumbs
salt and pepper to taste
1 c. all-purpose flour
2 to 3 T. oil
10-3/4 oz. can cream of
  mushroom soup

Mix together beef, egg, onion, cheese, catsup, milk, cracker crumbs, salt and pepper. Shape into 8 patties; dredge in flour. Heat oil in a large skillet over medium heat; brown patties on both sides. Arrange patties in a slow cooker alternately with soup. Cover and cook on high setting for 3 to 4 hours.

"Fried" ice cream is a festive dessert after Mexican Burgers.
Roll scoops of ice cream in a mixture of crushed frosted flake
cereal and cinnamon. Garnish with a drizzle of honey and a
dollop of whipped topping. They'll ask for seconds!

Mexican Burgers

1 avocado, pitted, peeled
    and diced
1 plum tomato, diced
2 green onions, chopped
1 to 2 t. lime juice
1-1/4 lbs. ground beef
1 egg, beaten
3/4 c. to 1 c. nacho-flavored
    tortilla chips, crushed

1/4 c. fresh cilantro, chopped
1/2 t. chili powder
1/2 t. ground cumin
salt and pepper to taste
1-1/4 c. shredded Pepper Jack
    cheese
5 hamburger buns, split

Mix together avocado, tomato, onions and lime juice; mash slightly and set aside. Combine beef, egg, chips and seasonings in a large bowl. Form into 5 patties; grill to desired doneness, turning to cook on both sides. Sprinkle cheese over burgers; grill until melted. Serve on buns; spread with avocado mixture.

If you let raw potatoes sit in a bowl of cold water for half an hour, they'll be crisper when you whip up a batch of homemade French fries.

Make-Ahead Pizza Burgers

Makes 20 servings

1 lb. ground beef
1 onion, chopped
1/2 green pepper, chopped
2 6-inch pepperoni sticks, ground
   or finely chopped
16-oz. jar pizza sauce
1 c. shredded mozzarella cheese

4 t. dried oregano or basil
1/8 t. garlic salt
Optional: 4-oz. can sliced
   mushrooms, drained
1/4 c. butter, softened
20 mini sandwich buns, split

In a skillet over medium heat, brown beef, onion and green pepper; drain. Stir in remaining ingredients except butter and buns; cook for several minutes, until cheese melts. Brush butter over cut sides of buns. Divide beef mixture among the bun bottoms; add tops. Burgers may be served immediately, or wrapped individually in aluminum foil and placed in the freezer. To serve if frozen: thaw in refrigerator overnight. Bake foil-wrapped burgers at 350 degrees for 15 to 20 minutes, until heated through.

Serve chilled beverages in old-fashioned Mason jars!
Setting the jars inside wire drink carriers makes it
easy to tote them from kitchen to picnic table.

Special Hamburger Sauce

Makes 12 servings

1 c. mayonnaise
1/3 c. creamy French salad
    dressing
1/4 c. sweet pickle relish

1 T. sugar
1 t. dried, minced onion
salt and pepper to taste

Combine all ingredients in a bowl; stir well. Cover and refrigerate up to one week. Serve over grilled burgers.

Place browned ground beef or turkey in a colander
and run hot water over it. Excess fat will rinse
right off with no loss in flavor.

Mom's Turkey Burgers

Makes 4 to 6 servings

1 lb. ground turkey
1 onion, chopped
1 to 2 T. oil
10-3/4 oz. can chicken gumbo
    soup

2 T. mustard
1 T. catsup
1/2 t. salt
4 to 6 hamburger buns, split

In a skillet over medium heat, brown turkey and onion in oil; drain. Add remaining ingredients except buns. Mix together and cook until heated through. Serve turkey mixture on hamburger buns.

Put a few extra burgers on the grill, then pop into buns, wrap individually and freeze. Later, just reheat in the microwave for quick meals...they'll taste freshly grilled!

Dagwood Burgers

Makes 12 to 15 sandwiches

2 lbs. lean ground beef
1 lb. ground Italian pork sausage
2 c. dry bread crumbs
1 onion, chopped
1/2 c. barbecue sauce

1 egg, beaten
1.35-oz. pkg. onion soup mix
1 t. jalapeño pepper, diced
salt and pepper to taste
12 to 15 hamburger buns, split

Mix all ingredients except salt, pepper and buns in a very large bowl.
Form into 12 to 15 patties; sprinkle with salt and pepper. Place on a
charcoal grill or in a skillet over medium heat. Cook burgers to desired
doneness. Serve on buns.

Have some hometown fun...turn your dining room into
a soda shoppe! Group round tables with vintage-style chairs,
then top each table with a checkered table cloth. Give your
"customers" whimsical menus featuring dinner specials that
include burgers, fries, shakes, malts and sundaes!

Hero Burgers

Makes 4 servings

1-1/2 lbs. ground beef
10-3/4 oz. can tomato soup
1/3 c. onion, finely chopped
1 T. mustard
1 T. Worcestershire sauce
1 t. prepared horseradish

1 t. salt
1 loaf French bread, halved
   lengthwise and toasted
2 tomatoes, sliced
2 c. shredded Cheddar cheese

In a bowl, combine beef, soup, onion, mustard, sauce, horseradish and salt. Spread mixture on bottom half of bread, covering edges completely. Broil 4 to 5 inches from heat source for 10 to 12 minutes. Top with tomatoes and cheese; broil for 5 additional minutes or until cheese is melted. Cover with top half of bread. Cut into 3-inch slices and serve.

Remember chocolate colas? Go ahead and treat yourself
to this soda-shop specialty...a tall glass of cola
with a squirt of chocolate syrup stirred in!

Broiled Hamburger Sandwich

Makes 4 servings

1 lb. lean ground beef
8-oz. pkg. shredded Cheddar
    cheese
1 t. Worcestershire sauce

1 t. browning and seasoning
    sauce
1 t. salt
4 slices French bread, toasted

In a bowl, combine beef, cheese, sauces and salt; mix well. Spread mixture over one side of each bread slice. Place on an ungreased baking sheet. Broil for about 5 to 8 minutes, until beef is cooked through and cheese is melted.

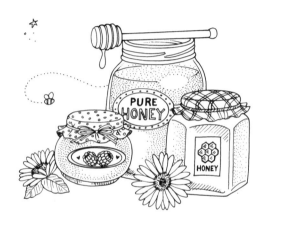

Honey comes in lots of flavor varieties. Seek out
a local beekeeper at the farmers' market and try
a few samples...you may find a new favorite!

Quick Hot & Sweet Mustard

Makes 1/2 cup

1/3 c. brown mustard seed
3 T. cider vinegar
1 T. olive oil

1/2 t. honey
1/8 t. dried tarragon

Grind mustard seeds in a spice grinder; place in a small mixing bowl. Add remaining ingredients; stir until smooth and thick. Refrigerate in an airtight container until serving.

Need to peel tomatoes in a hurry? Simply drop them into boiling water, then submerge them in cold water... the skins will slip right off.

Garden-Fresh Catsup

Makes 2, one-quart jars

3 lbs. tomatoes, peeled
   and chopped
1 onion, peeled and diced
1/2 c. vinegar
1/2 c. sugar
1 t. salt

1 t. paprika
1 t. pepper
1/2 t. nutmeg
1/4 t. ground cloves
1 T. chili sauce
2 one-quart wide-mouth jars

Mix together all ingredients in a large stockpot; bring to a boil and let simmer for 20 minutes. Remove from heat and let cool. Ladle into jars. Store in refrigerator up to 2 weeks.

Invite friends over for a cookout before the big game.
Begin with invitations made of felt in the shape of pennants
or use a permanent marker to write party information on
small plastic footballs.

Country Friends Chili Burgers

Serves 4 to 6

1 lb. ground beef
1 10-1/2 oz. can condensed bean
    with bacon soup

1/2 c. catsup
1 t. chili powder
4 to 6 buns, split and toasted

Brown beef in large skillet; drain. Stir in soup, catsup and chili powder.
Let simmer 5 to 10 minutes, adding water if more "juice" is desired.
Spoon onto buns.

Don't put your grill away when summer's over! Fall can be
the greatest time of the year for cookouts...the bugs are gone
and the cooler weather makes for perfect outdoor suppers.

Black Bean Turkey Burgers

Makes 6 servings

1-1/4 lbs. ground turkey
3/4 c. canned black beans,
    drained, rinsed and lightly
    mashed
1 c. tortilla chips, crushed

1 T. chili powder
1 T. ground cumin
salt and pepper to taste
6 hamburger buns, split

In a large bowl, combine turkey, beans, tortilla chips and seasonings.
Mix well and form into 6 patties. Grill over medium-high heat for 6 to
8 minutes per side. Serve burgers on buns, topped with a scoop of
Avocado & Onion Slaw.

Avocado & Onion Slaw:

3 T. mayonnaise
1 T. vinegar
1/4 t. salt

1 avocado, halved, pitted
    and cubed
1/2 c. onion, thinly sliced

Mix together mayonnaise, vinegar and salt until well combined. Stir in
avocado and onion.

The promise of a savory 7-League Pizza Burger is all
it takes to get kids motivated for a service project!
The little time it takes to help weed a neighbor's garden or
plant flowers around the chapel pays big rewards...kids learn
to give of their time and care for others.

7-League Pizza Burger

Makes 5 servings

1 lb. ground beef
1/3 c. grated Parmesan cheese
6-oz. can tomato paste
1 t. dried oregano
1 t. salt
1/8 t. pepper
1 loaf French bread, halved
    lengthwise

1/4 c. sliced black olives
3 tomatoes, peeled and thinly
    sliced
5 slices sharp pasteurized process
    cheese
1/4 c. onion, finely chopped

Combine beef, cheese, tomato paste, oregano, salt and pepper. Spread evenly onto both bread halves. Broil about 5 inches from heat source for 12 minutes, or until beef is no longer pink in the center. Arrange tomato and cheese slices alternately down the center of each half. Broil for an additional one to 2 minutes, until cheese starts to melt. Slice each half into 4 to 5 pieces.

A backyard camp-out is a fun summertime get-together for kids...staple a bag of mini marshmallows or trail mix to invitations! Fun activities like a scavenger hunt, shadow puppets, a nighttime flashlight walk and stargazing will be sure to keep the fun going all evening long.

All-American Cheeseburgers

Makes 10 sandwiches

1 lb. ground beef, browned
    and drained
3 T. catsup
2 t. mustard

2 c. pasteurized process cheese
    spread, cubed
10 hamburger buns, split

Place beef in a slow cooker; add catsup and mustard, mixing well. Top with cubed cheese. Cover and cook on low setting for 3 to 4 hours. Gently stir beef mixture; spoon onto buns.

Stop pesky ants from crashing your picnic! Sprinkle salt,
crushed chalk or talcum powder in a line around the
picnic table...they won't cross that line.

Cheeseburger Roll-Ups

Serves 6 to 8

2 lbs. ground beef
3/4 c. soft bread crumbs
1/2 c. onion, minced
2 eggs, beaten
1-1/2 t. salt
1-1/2 t. pepper

12-oz. pkg. shredded Cheddar
   cheese
6 to 8 sandwich buns, split
Garnish: catsup, mustard
   and lettuce

In a large bowl, combine beef, bread crumbs, onion, eggs, salt and pepper; mix well. Pat out into an 18-inch by 14-inch rectangle on a piece of wax paper. Spread cheese over beef mixture, leaving a 3/4-inch border around edges. Roll up jelly-roll fashion starting at short edge. Press ends to seal. Place on a lightly greased 15"x10" jelly-roll pan. Bake at 350 degrees for one hour, or until internal temperature on a meat thermometer reaches 160 degrees. Let stand at least 10 minutes before slicing. Slice and serve on buns; garnish as desired.

Generally, you should close the cover on the grill when
you are cooking large pieces of food or slow grilling; swing the
lid open when food is cut up into small chunks or thin pieces.

Denise's Pizza Burgers

Serves 8 to 10

2-1/2 lbs. ground beef
1/4 c. bread crumbs
1 T. dried basil
1 T. Italian seasoning
1/2 t. pepper
10 to 12 slices pepperoni,
    quartered

1/2 c. shredded mozzarella cheese
8-oz. jar pizza sauce, divided
8 to 10 slices mozzarella or
    provolone cheese
8 to 10 kaiser rolls, split

In a bowl, mix beef, bread crumbs, seasonings, pepperoni and cheese; add 1/4 cup pizza sauce. Shape into 8 to 10 patties. Grill on a hot grill to desired doneness. Warm remaining pizza sauce. Serve burgers on rolls, topping each with cheese and a spoonful of pizza sauce.

A tasty apple coleslaw goes well with German Burgers.
Simply toss together a large bag of coleslaw mix and
a chopped Granny Smith apple. Stir in coleslaw dressing
to desired consistency.

German Burgers

1-1/2 lbs. ground beef
1/2 c. soft pumpernickel bread
   crumbs
2 T. beer or beef broth
1 T. mustard
1/2 t. caraway seed
1/2 t. salt

1/8 t. pepper
6 slices Swiss cheese
6 pumpernickel sandwich
   buns, split
14-1/2 oz. can sauerkraut,
   drained
Garnish: additional mustard

In a large bowl, combine all ingredients except cheese, buns and sauerkraut. Mix gently and form into 6 patties. Grill or pan-fry patties to desired doneness, about 10 to 15 minutes, turning halfway through. Top with cheese; let stand until cheese melts. Grill buns, if desired. Serve burgers on buns; top with sauerkraut and mustard.

Only using part of an onion? The remaining half will
stay fresh for weeks when rubbed with butter or oil
and stored in the refrigerator.

Zesty Onion Relish

Makes 10 to 12 servings

2 lbs. large onions, sliced thick
1/4 c. canola oil
3 T. balsamic vinegar

2 T. brown sugar, packed
1/4 t. cayenne pepper

Lightly brush onion slices on each side with oil. Place onions on grill and cook over low heat for 15 minutes or until tender and golden. Flip onions to brown each side, coating again with oil as needed. Remove onions from grill and allow to cool. Chop onions and set aside. Simmer vinegar and brown sugar in a saucepan over low heat. Cook and stir until sugar has dissolved; pour over onions. Sprinkle cayenne pepper over top and stir again. Serve warm, refrigerating any leftovers.

Hosting a barbecue will guarantee a big turnout of friends & neighbors! Load grills with chicken, ribs, brats, burgers and hot dogs, then ask guests to bring a favorite side dish or dessert to share. Add a game of softball and it's a winner!

Backyard Big South-of-the-Border Burgers

Makes 6 servings

4-oz. can chopped green chiles, drained
1/4 c. picante sauce
12 round buttery crackers, crushed
4-1/2 t. chili powder
1 T. ground cumin
1/2 t. smoke-flavored cooking sauce
1/2 t. salt
1/2 t. pepper
2 lbs. lean ground beef
1/2 lb. ground pork sausage
6 slices Pepper Jack cheese
6 sesame seed hamburger buns, split
Garnish: lettuce leaves, sliced tomato

In a large bowl, combine first 8 ingredients. Crumble beef and sausage over mixture and mix well. Form into 6 patties. Grill, covered, over medium heat for 5 to 7 minutes on each side, until no longer pink in the center. Top with cheese. Grill until cheese is melted. Grill buns, cut-side down, for one to 2 minutes, until toasted. Serve burgers on buns, garnished as desired.

An ice cream social is welcome relief from the summer heat.
Set up an ice cream stand with big scoops of ice cream and
lots of toppings...nuts, whipped cream, bananas and homemade
root beer for creamy floats.

Delicious Patty Melts

2 to 3 T. butter, softened and
 divided
1 onion, thinly sliced
1 lb. ground beef, formed into
 4 thin patties

seasoned salt and pepper to taste
8 slices rye bread
8 slices Swiss cheese

Melt one tablespoon butter in a skillet over medium heat; add onion.
Cook for 10 to 15 minutes, until onion is golden and caramelized.
Meanwhile, season beef patties with salt and pepper. On a griddle over
medium heat, brown patties for about 6 minutes on each side, until no
longer pink in center. Wipe griddle clean with a paper towel. Spread
remaining butter on one side of each bread slice; place 4 slices butter-side
down on hot griddle. Top each bread slice with a cheese slice, a beef
patty, 1/4 of onion, another cheese slice and another bread slice, butter-
side up. Cook sandwiches over medium-low heat until golden on both
sides and cheese is melted, about 5 minutes.

A great gift for Dad! Give a platter of Dad's Wimpy Burgers with a coupon good for an indoor tailgating party...uninterrupted football coverage complete with his favorite snacks and drinks.

Dad's Wimpy Burgers

Makes 6 to 8 servings

2 lbs. ground beef
1/2 c. catsup
1 egg, beaten
1 onion, chopped

1 t. salt
1 c. Italian-flavored dry bread
    crumbs
6 to 8 hamburger buns, split

In a large bowl, combine beef, catsup, egg, onion and salt; mix well. Form into 6 to 8 patties. Place bread crumbs in a shallow pan. Pat each side of patties in crumbs until coated. Place patties in a lightly greased 13"x9" baking pan. Bake, uncovered, at 350 degrees for 20 to 25 minutes, flipping patties after 8 minutes. Patties may also be pan-fried in a lightly greased skillet over medium heat. Cook on each side for 6 to 8 minutes, until lightly browned. Serve on buns.

Burgers don't have to be ordinary...try making them with ground turkey, chicken or even ground sausage. Season them with Italian, Mexican, Thai, Southwest or Mediterranean blends easily found at the meat counter.

Chicken Burgers

Makes 4 to 6 sandwiches

1 lb. ground chicken
1 onion, chopped
1/8 t. garlic powder
1/4 c. fresh bread crumbs
3 T. chicken broth

1 t. Dijon mustard
1 t. salt-free vegetable seasoning
   salt
pepper to taste
4 to 6 hamburger buns, split

Combine all ingredients except buns in a large bowl. Stir lightly with a fork until well blended. Shape into 4 to 6 burgers. Heat a lightly oiled skillet over medium heat. Cook burgers in skillet for 6 to 8 minutes per side, until no longer pink in the center. Serve on buns.

When burgers, hot dogs, tacos or baked potatoes are on the menu, set up a topping bar with bowls of shredded cheese, catsup or salsa, crispy bacon and other yummy stuff. Everyone can just help themselves to their favorite toppings!

8 Great Burgers

1 lb. ground beef
1 lb. ground pork sausage
2 T. Worcestershire sauce
1/2 c. grated Parmesan cheese
1/3 t. pepper
8 hamburger buns, split
Garnish: lettuce, sliced tomato,
   sliced onion

Combine beef, pork, sauce, cheese and pepper in a large bowl. Mix well; form into 8 patties. Grill burgers to desired doneness, about 5 to 6 minutes per side. Serve on buns with favorite toppings.

Before marinating burgers, chicken or chops, pour some
marinade into a plastic squeeze bottle for easy basting while
the meat sizzles away on the grill...how clever!

Devilishly Good Burgers

Makes 4 servings

1 lb. ground beef
2 T. catsup
1 T. onion, chopped
2 t. mustard

1 t. red steak sauce
1 t. seasoned salt
1/2 t. pepper
4 hamburger buns, split

In a large bowl, combine all ingredients except buns. Mix well; form into 4 burgers. Cover and refrigerate for about 8 hours to allow flavors to blend. Grill or fry burgers to desired doneness. Serve burgers on buns.

Grill some veggies alongside the meat! Brush olive oil over sliced squash, potatoes, peppers or eggplant and grill until tender and golden. You may be surprised how sweet and delicious they are.

Hamburger "Cupcakes"

Makes one dozen

12 slices white or whole-wheat
    bread
1/4 to 1/2 c. butter, softened
1 lb. ground beef
1/2 c. onion, chopped
10-3/4 oz. can cream of
    mushroom soup

1/2 c. shredded sharp Cheddar
    cheese
salt, pepper and garlic powder
    to taste
Optional: additional cheese

Cut off the crusts from each bread slice; cut the crusts into cubes and
set aside. Spread butter over one side of each bread slice. Press bread,
butter-side down, into muffin cups. In a bowl, combine crust cubes and
remaining ingredients; mix well. Divide mixture among muffin cups. Top
with a little more cheese, if desired. Bake at 375 degrees for 35 to
40 minutes, until no longer pink in the center.

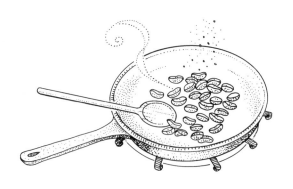

Toasting nuts adds lots of flavor...with no oil needed.
Place nuts in a dry skillet over medium heat. Cook and stir until
lightly golden, about 3 minutes. Cool completely before
adding to recipes.

Mom's Nutty Burgers

Serves 4

3 slices whole-wheat bread, torn
1 c. milk
1 egg
1 slice onion
1 carrot, peeled and diced

1 stalk celery, diced
2 c. chopped walnuts
1 t. salt
1/4 c. butter
Optional: 8 buns, split

In a blender, process bread for several seconds until crumbs form.
Remove crumbs to a bowl. Add milk, egg, vegetables, nuts and salt to
blender. Process about 30 seconds, until chopped. Add to crumbs; mix
well and form into 8 patties. Heat butter in a skillet. Cook patties for
5 minutes per side, flipping carefully, until golden. Serve on buns,
if desired.

Stuffed burgers turn ordinary into an extraordinary dinner!
Form a thin patty and top with a sprinkle of cheese, roasted garlic,
bacon crumbles, salsa or fresh herbs. Place another thin patty
on top and carefully seal the edges. Grill as usual and enjoy!

Brie-Stuffed Burgers

Makes 6 servings

2 lbs. ground turkey
6 cubes Brie cheese, 1"x1"x1/2"
2 T. olive oil, divided
salt and pepper to taste
1 tart apple, cored and thickly
   sliced crosswise

6 multi-grain rolls, split and
   toasted
Optional: cranberry mustard

Form turkey into 6 thick patties. Hollow out center of each and place a cheese cube inside; press meat around cheese to cover. Brush one tablespoon oil over burgers; sprinkle with salt and pepper. Grill over medium-high heat to desired doneness. Brush remaining oil over apple slices; grill (or sauté in a skillet) until golden. Place burgers on rolls; top with apple slices and a dollop of cranberry mustard, if desired.

Pack some Hamburger Seasoning Mix into a barbecue gift bag! Cut 2 back pockets from a pair of old blue jeans, arrange on the front of a white gift bag and secure with hot glue. Slip a sassy red bandanna in one pocket and a gift card in the other.

Hamburger Seasoning Mix

Makes 2-1/2 cups

1-1/4 t. pepper
3 T. onion powder
1 T. garlic powder
1 t. salt

1-2/3 c. powdered milk
1/3 c. dried, minced onion
3-1/2 T. beef bouillon granules
2 T. dried parsley

Combine ingredients; store in an airtight container.

To use:

Add one to 2 tablespoons Hamburger Seasoning Mix to one pound ground beef before forming into patties to grill.

Need just a dash of lemon or lime juice? Pierce the fruit
with an ice pick, squeeze out as much as needed and
return it to the refrigerator until next use.

Key West Burgers

1 lb. ground beef
3 T. Key lime juice
1/4 c. fresh cilantro, chopped

salt and pepper to taste
hamburger buns, split and toasted
Garnish: lettuce

In a bowl, combine beef, lime juice, cilantro, salt and pepper. Form beef mixture into 4 patties. Spray a large skillet with non-stick vegetable spray. Cook patties over medium heat for 6 minutes. Flip patties, cover skillet and cook for another 6 minutes. Place lettuce on bottom halves of buns and top with patties. Add Creamy Burger Spread onto bun tops and close sandwiches.

Creamy Burger Spread:

8-oz. pkg. cream cheese, softened
8-oz. container sour cream

3 green onion tops, chopped

Combine all ingredients until completely blended. Cover and refrigerate at least 15 minutes.

Fruit kabobs are a sweet ending to any meal. Arrange chunks
of pineapple and banana, plump strawberries and kiwi slices
on skewers. For a creamy dipping sauce, blend together
1/2 cup each of cream cheese and marshmallow creme.

Island Burgers

Makes 6 to 8 sandwiches

1 lb. ground beef
1 lb. ground turkey
Optional: 1.35-oz. pkg. onion
    soup mix
seasoned salt to taste

6 to 8 hamburger buns, split and
    toasted
1/2 lb. deli shaved ham, warmed
6 to 8 pineapple slices
1/2 c. French salad dressing

In a bowl, mix together beef and turkey; blend in soup mix, if desired. Form into 6 to 8 burgers. Place on a broiling pan or grill; sprinkle on both sides with seasoned salt. Broil or grill to desired doneness. Serve burgers on toasted buns, topped with ham, a slice of pineapple and a drizzle of salad dressing.

For thick burgers that cook up more quickly and evenly, press your thumb into the center of each patty to form a dime-size hole. The hole will close as the burgers brown.

Marty's Special Burgers

Makes 4 sandwiches

1 lb. lean ground beef
2/3 c. crumbled feta or
    blue cheese
1/2 c. bread crumbs
1 egg, beaten

1/2 t. salt
1/4 t. pepper
4 to 6 cherry tomatoes, halved
4 hamburger buns, split

Mix together all ingredients except buns; form into 4 burgers. Grill over high heat to desired doneness, flipping to cook on both sides. Serve on buns.

For a quick & tasty side, slice fresh tomatoes in half and sprinkle with minced garlic, Italian seasoning and grated Parmesan cheese. Broil until tomatoes are tender, about 5 minutes...scrumptious!

Spinach Cheeseburgers

2 lbs. ground beef
1 c. shredded mozzarella cheese
1.35-oz. pkg. onion soup mix
10-oz. pkg. frozen chopped
    spinach, thawed and drained

8 hamburger buns, split and
    lightly toasted

Combine all ingredients except buns in a large bowl; shape into 8 patties.
Grill or broil to desired doneness. Serve on toasted buns.

Next time you finish a jar of dill pickles, use the leftover juice
to make some crunchy, tangy pickled veggies! Cut up fresh
carrots, green peppers, celery and other favorite veggies,
add them to the pickle juice and refrigerate for a few days.

Garlic Dill Pickles

Makes 3 jars

9 c. pickling cucumbers, sliced
3 1-quart canning jars and lids,
    sterilized
3 grape leaves
3 t. dill seed

3 cloves garlic
6 c. white vinegar
3 qts. water
1-1/2 c. salt

Pack cucumbers evenly between sterilized jars, leaving 1/2-inch headspace. To each jar add one grape leaf, one teaspoon dill seed and one clove garlic. Combine remaining ingredients in a large saucepan over medium heat. Cook and stir until hot and salt is dissolved. Pour vinegar evenly into hot sterilized jars, leaving 1/2-inch headspace. Wipe rims; secure with lids and rings. Process in a boiling water bath for 15 minutes; set jars on a towel to cool. Check for seals.

To really speed up any recipe with crisply cooked bacon,
purchase pre-cooked bacon. Just snip and add to salads
or leave whole for sandwiches and burgers.

Bacon & Blue Cheese Stuffed Burgers

Makes 4 burgers

1-1/2 lbs. ground beef
1 T. Worcestershire sauce
2 T. Dijon mustard
1/2 t. pepper
4 to 6 slices bacon, crisply cooked
    and crumbled

4-oz. container crumbled blue
    cheese
4 hamburger buns, split and
    toasted
Garnish: sliced red onion, sliced
    tomato, lettuce leaves

Combine beef, Worcestershire sauce, mustard and pepper. Mix lightly and form into 8 1/4-inch thick patties. Stir together bacon and blue cheese; set aside 1/3 of mixture for topping. Spoon remaining mixture onto centers of 4 patties. Top with remaining 4 patties; press edges together to seal. Grill over medium-high heat to desired doneness, 4 to 6 minutes per side, topping with reserved bacon mixture when nearly done. Serve burgers on toasted buns, garnished as desired.

Fresh corn on the cob is always a favorite summer side dish.
Make buttering ears a snap...add melted butter to a glass
tall enough for dipping ears, one at a time.

Smoky Bacon-Gouda Burgers

Makes 4 servings

1/4 c. onion, finely chopped
6 slices bacon, cut into 1/2-inch
    pieces, crisply cooked and
    1 T. drippings reserved
2 T. olive oil
1-3/4 c. onion, thinly sliced
1/4 c. steak sauce
1-1/2 lbs. ground beef sirloin

2 t. Worcestershire sauce
1 t. hot pepper sauce
1 T. steak seasoning
4 slices smoked Gouda cheese
4 kaiser rolls or onion rolls,
    split and toasted
Optional: crisply cooked bacon,
    sliced tomato, lettuce leaves

In a skillet over medium heat, cook chopped onion in reserved drippings
until soft, 2 to 3 minutes. Combine with bacon in a small bowl; set aside.
Heat oil in skillet; add sliced onion and sauté, covered, until golden,
about 10 minutes. Place in another bowl; stir in steak sauce and set
aside. In a large bowl, combine beef, remaining sauces, seasoning and
onion-bacon mixture; mix lightly and form into 4 patties. Grill over
medium-high heat to desired doneness, topping with cheese slices when
nearly done. Serve burgers on toasted rolls, topped with sliced onion
mixture and other toppings as desired.

Grill a juicy ripe peach for an easy dessert. Brush peach halves
with melted butter and place cut-side down on a hot grill.
Cook for several minutes, until tender and golden.
Drizzle with honey...delicious!

Grilled Summer Burgers

Makes 4 to 5 sandwiches

1 lb. ground beef
1/2 c. onion, chopped
2 T. green pepper, finely chopped
3 T. catsup
1-1/2 T. prepared horseradish

2 t. mustard
1 t. salt
pepper to taste
4 to 5 hamburger buns, split

Combine all ingredients except buns. Shape into patties. Broil or grill for 5 minutes. Flip patties and cook the other side to desired doneness. Place on buns to serve.

A sweet treat for a lazy summer afternoon...ice cream floats!
Frosty glasses filled with scoops of vanilla ice cream
topped with root beer, red or orange soda will be a hit.

Nightmares

1 lb. ground beef
1/2 c. onion, chopped
salt and pepper to taste

15-oz. can chili without beans
8 hamburger buns, split
8 slices American cheese

In a skillet over medium heat, brown beef with onion, salt and pepper; drain. Add chili and mix well; remove from heat. Divide the beef mixture among the bun bottoms; top each with a slice of cheese and bun top. Wrap each bun in aluminum foil; place on a baking sheet. Bake at 350 degrees for 15 to 20 minutes. May be made in advance and frozen unbaked. To serve, bake frozen sandwiches for about 45 minutes.

Delight the kids with super-simple ice cream sandwiches!
Place a scoop of softened ice cream on the flat bottom of
one side of a cookie. Top with another cookie, bottom-side down;
press gently. Enjoy right away, or wrap and freeze for
up to one week.

County Fair Maidrites

Makes 20 to 25 servings

5 lbs. ground beef
1/2 c. onion, diced
2 T. salt
2 t. pepper
5 c. catsup
1/3 c. mustard

1/4 c. quick-cooking oats,
    uncooked
3 T. brown sugar, packed
2-1/2 t. Worcestershire sauce
20 to 25 hamburger buns, split

Brown beef in a very large skillet over medium heat; drain. Add onion, salt and pepper; cook until onion is transparent. Add remaining ingredients except buns; stir and simmer until heated through. Spoon onto buns.

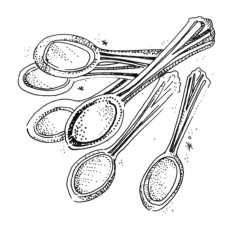

Keep an eye out for vintage silver spoons at flea markets...
oh-so clever tied onto giftable jars of Olive Burger Topping,
salsa, mustard or relish.

Olive Burger Topping

8-oz. pkg. cream cheese, softened
1 c. sliced green olives with
   pimentos
6 T. olive juice

1/2 onion, finely chopped
Optional: chopped green chiles
   to taste

Mix together all ingredients, stirring well to blend in olive juice. Cover and chill at least 2 hours. Serve on grilled burgers as desired.

For a speedy side with Tex-Mex flair, dress up a 16-ounce can of refried beans...it's easy! Sauté 2 seeded and diced pickled jalapeños, 2 chopped cloves garlic and 1/4 cup chopped onion in 2 tablespoons bacon drippings. Add beans, heat through and stir in 1/2 teaspoon ground cumin.

Black Bean Burgers

Makes 4 sandwiches

15-oz. can black beans, drained
    and rinsed
1 onion, chopped
1 egg, beaten
1/2 c. dry bread crumbs

1 t. garlic salt
1 t. cayenne pepper
4 whole-wheat buns, split
Garnish: sliced tomatoes,
    Swiss cheese slices

Place black beans and onion in a food processor; process to a mashed consistency. Transfer to a bowl; mix in egg, bread crumbs and seasonings. Form into 4 burgers; cook on a grill or in a skillet for about 5 minutes on each side, until golden. Serve on buns; garnish as desired.

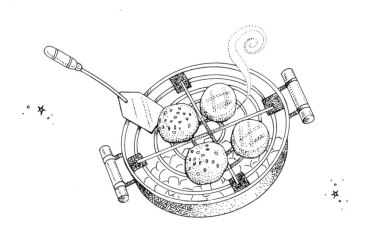

Burgers are even more mouthwatering when served on toasty grilled buns! Simply place buns split-side down on the grill for one to 2 minutes, until golden.

Alberta Prairie Burgers

Makes 4 to 6 sandwiches

1 lb. ground beef
1/2 c. quick-cooking oats,
    uncooked
1/4 c. light sour cream
1/4 c. mushrooms, minced
1 onion, finely chopped
3 cloves garlic, minced

1 T. Dijon mustard
1 T. fresh parsley, chopped
1 t. dried oregano
1 t. dried thyme
1/4 t. salt
1/4 t. pepper
4 to 6 hamburger buns, split

Combine all ingredients except buns; mix lightly, blending well. Form
into 4 to 6 patties, one to 2 inches thick. Grill on a lightly oiled grill
over medium heat for 5 to 7 minutes per side, flipping once, to desired
doneness. May broil or pan-fry if preferred. Serve on buns.

Bright bandanas make colorful napkins for any barbecue.
Tie one around each person's set of utensils. After the
party, just toss them in the wash.

Open-Faced Lone Star Burgers

Makes 6 servings

1/4 c. onion, chopped
2 cloves garlic, minced
1/4 t. dried thyme
1-1/2 c. shredded Colby Jack
    cheese, divided
1-1/2 lbs. ground beef

6 slices frozen garlic Texas toast
8-oz. can tomato sauce
1 T. brown sugar, packed
1 t. Worcestershire sauce
1 t. steak sauce

In a large bowl, combine onion, garlic, thyme and one cup cheese. Crumble beef over top and mix well. Form into 6 oval-shaped patties. In a large skillet, cook patties over medium heat for 5 to 6 minutes per side, to desired doneness. Meanwhile, prepare toast according to package directions. Drain burgers; set aside and keep warm. Add remaining ingredients to the skillet. Bring to a boil; cook and stir for 2 minutes, or until slightly thickened. Return burgers to skillet; turn to coat. Sprinkle with remaining cheese. Serve burgers on toast.

Having a picnic on a breezy day? Cast-off clip earrings make sparkly tablecloth weights...simply clip 'em to each corner of the cloth.

Tex-Mex Burgers

Makes 8 burgers

2 lbs. ground beef
1 c. shredded Cheddar cheese
1/2 c. onion, grated

1/2 c. salsa
2 to 3 cups tortilla chips, crushed
8 sandwich buns, split

In a bowl, combine all ingredients except buns; shape into patties. Grill over medium heat to desired doneness. Serve on buns.

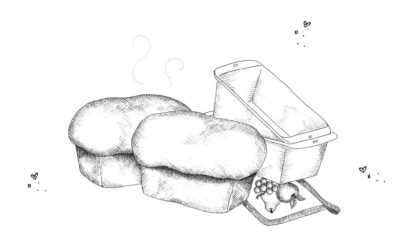

Grandma's little secret...kneading bread dough is a
fun way to get rid of stress! Be sure to knead the dough
as long as the recipe states, until the dough is silky smooth.
You'll be rewarded with moist, tender buns or bread.

Homemade Burger Buns   *Makes 8 to 12 buns*

2 T. active dry yeast
1 c. plus 2 T. warm water
1/3 c. oil
1/4 c. sugar

1 egg, beaten
1 t. salt
3 to 3-1/2 c. all-purpose flour
Optional: melted butter

In a large bowl, dissolve yeast in very warm water, 110 to 115 degrees.
Stir in oil and sugar; let stand for 5 minutes. Mix in egg and salt; stir in
enough flour to form a soft dough. Turn onto a floured surface. Knead for
3 to 5 minutes, until smooth and elastic. Divide dough into 8 to 12 balls.
Place on greased baking sheets, 3 inches apart. Cover and let stand for
10 minutes. Brush with butter, if desired. Bake at 425 degrees for 8 to
12 minutes, until golden. Cool buns on wire racks.

INDEX

INDEX

Our Story

Back in 1984, we were next-door neighbors raising our families in the little town of Delaware, Ohio. Two moms with small children, we were looking for a way to do what we loved and stay home with the kids too. We had always shared a love of home cooking and making memories with family & friends and so, after many a conversation over the backyard fence, **Gooseberry Patch** was born.

We put together our first catalog at our kitchen tables, enlisting the help of our loved ones wherever we could. From that very first mailing, we found an immediate connection with many of our customers and it wasn't long before we began receiving letters, photos and recipes from these new friends. In 1992, we put together our very first cookbook, compiled from hundreds of these recipes and, the rest, as they say, is history.

Hard to believe it's been over 25 years since those kitchen-table days! From that original little **Gooseberry Patch** family, we've grown to include an amazing group of creative folks who love cooking, decorating and creating as much as we do. Today, we're best known for our homestyle, family-friendly cookbooks, now recognized as national bestsellers.

One thing's for sure, we couldn't have done it without our friends all across the country. Each year, we're honored to turn thousands of your recipes into our collectible cookbooks. Our hope is that each book captures the stories and heart of all of you who have shared with us. Whether you've been with us since the beginning or are just discovering us, welcome to the **Gooseberry Patch** family!

Visit our website anytime
www.gooseberrypatch.com

Email

Jo Ann & Vickie

1·800·854·6673